Poetry of Presence

Verses for Life in the Now

By Dean Jackson

lifeinthenow.com

@deanjacksonnow

DEPTHS OF HER SOUL

She dances to the songs in her head,
Speaks with the rhythm of her heart,
And loves from the depths of her soul.

BUTTERFLY

When she transformed into a butterfly,
the caterpillars spoke not of her beauty,
but of her weirdness.
They wanted her to change back
into what she always had been.

But she had wings.

ARTIST

Each now is a new life beginning,
a blank canvas, fresh, clean, alive,
and you are the artist.

TWO SOULS

Two souls looked out at the world
and saw the same thing.

One was filled with joy.
The other was filled with pain.

It's not the thing we look upon
that paints our point of view,
but the heart through which we see it
that gives our world its hue.

GIFT FROM A CHILD

When a child gives you a gift,
even if it is a rock they just picked up,
exude gratitude.
It may be the only thing they have to give,
and they have chosen to give it to you.

MAGICIAN

May you become a presence magician,
seeing beauty in the mess,
conjuring peace from the stress,
waiving the wand of forgiveness,
first over yourself.

LOST IN WORDS

I'm looking at her across the room,
book in hand,
arms pressing down the blanket
that wraps her body.
Lost in words,
but sensing my gaze,
she looks over the pages and smiles.
Then her eyes and mind
return to another world
while her heart stays
here with me.

SEARCHES

Ego searches the loveliest garden
to find a single thorn.
Spirit searches the most desolate desert
to find a single bloom.

SECRET

Meet me in the corridor of your soul.
Invite me to the hidden chambers.
Show me the light behind your eyes.
Teach me the rhythm of your blood.
You are the secret I crave to discover.

ONGOING CHOICE

Each moment brings the choice to
re-live, pre-live,
or live.

SOFT GAZE

Look upon another with soft gaze and
see them through the eyes of love.
Silently observe their darkness
and their light.
See them as they are
and not as you wish them to be,
and you will see them
for the first time.

SOMETHING NEW

Faced with inevitable change,
the choice was mine.
I could fight until
my spirit was weary,
or I could release all resistance
and create something new
in my changed world.

IT AND ALL

Whenever you come to it,
you will get it all.

No matter how long it takes,
or how many times you fall.

INSPIRATION

The wishes and dreams of many
move the winds of inspiration,
but only you can spread
your wings to fly.

KNOWING

I've come to know the reality of you.
Certainly not the details,
but the reality.

LOVE ANEW

Collapse into me and rest.
Release every muscle, every fear.
Melt your skin into mine.
Sink your thoughts in the
rhythmic waves of my breathing.
Sleep to the white noise of my heart.
Awaken to love anew.

AGE

If age is only a marker in time,
then we are simply drifting
to a certain and universal finish.

But if age is the death of wonder,
then we hold a power of life
not relinquished until our common end,
when exchanged for
something unimaginable.

PERSPECTIVE

No matter where I am
or what I'm going through,
there is a power inside me that
sees the situation as it is—
an illusion, temporary, passing—
and from this perspective
all can be well.

FLAWED

The more we talked,
The more imperfect
you appeared to be,
and each imperfection revealed
drew me nearer to
your flawed and
precious heart.

TRUCE

Declare an end
to the war in your mind.
You cannot be the conqueror
without also being the conquered.

Having won and lost,
you stand where you began,
weary from the fight.

Lay down the weapons
you wield against yourself
and accept your worthiness.

IDENTITY

Love is what you give.
Love is what you receive.
But mostly, love is what you are.

MELODY

Music is a power that
turns the currents of the mind,
steering them to thirsty ground,
the melody of sound and soul converging,
blending hearts from far away,
rediscovering passion long hidden,
words lifted from a page,
given life,
the song birds bow,
the spirits take note,
fear and regret are frozen in time,
and I am brought back to me,
to you.

TRADING

Just here,
trading memories for inspiration,
scripts for awakening,
depression for passion.

Just here,
in the light of this moment.

CIRCLE OF ANGELS

I see your dancing demons and the
circle of angels around them.
I see the steep cliffs from which
you have fallen and the light
you share with those on the path.
The crushing fists of misguided choices,
the blows and bruises
that would mark the end
for those of weaker will,
became your food and drink.
Feasting,
you set the table and invite in
those starving as you once were.

EXPRESSIONS

One of the greatest
expressions of love
is simply listening
without judgment
or thought of reply.

MORE

You are so much more than the
thoughts about who you are,
those stories born from
memory and fear,
cast upon us,
created by us,
distorted,
magnified,
recycled,
illusions.
So much more.

DIRECTION

To look honestly
at where I am this moment.
To confess honestly that
I alone am responsible
for my place at this moment.
To know with smiling hope in the
midst of this confession
that I alone have the power
to choose my next direction.

ONE DAY

One day,
you will leave the earth plane.

Then,
one day,
later,

the last person to remember you
will leave the earth plane.

Then,
there are only stories and pictures;
and, things created by you.

The stories will fade as their tellers
leave the earth plane.

The pictures will be lost to time.

And all that is left is what you created.

The things you created here,
on the earth plane,

one day.

LETTERS

We are all fine letters in the sand,
made with love by an unseen hand,
never knowing as time goes past,
which incoming wave will be our last.

So let us see the sand and sky,
and smell each breeze passing by,
and hear each bird, touch each shell,
and know inside that all is well.

EGO'S DISGUISES

Ego comes in many disguises,
pretending to be logic or even truth,
trying to convince of us of the
many ways to achieve enlightenment,
as spirit sits quietly,
knowing that enlightenment
is not a matter of doing,
but a magnificent consequence
of being.

TURNS

What lurks or lies
around the next corner,
the endless bends
as far as I see—
and beyond—
the unknowns
that haunt or thrill?

I do not know.

But in this moment,
only this moment,
I have the power
to choose my
next direction,
until I face
another corner
or bend,
and then the power
to choose again.

BEYOND

Things come from beyond,
light shines from within,
illumination—the order
of all things listening,
the vibration of source,
energy when all seems drained,
darkness without cause
when eyes are shut,
life when stillness reigns,
all the same,
appearing as many,
searching for ends of the endless,
and time when there is none,
reaching for elusive joy
disguised as form,
fading fingers shredding
the fog of many illusions,
mysteries not to be solved
on this plane,
a knowing without words,
giving reason to it all,
and born anew
we begin.

WALLS

These towering walls
you have built to protect
your heart do nothing more
than imprison your spirit.

Crush the walls that
have been crushing you.
Feel your heart pulse
and your spirit tingle.

TO LIVE

Whether I know the reason,
today, I will live or die,
so today I choose to live,
'til the choice is no longer mine.

PAST

The past is but a
collection of thoughts.
Its power over me
is up to me
for it is not me.

MAGIC

The highest form of magic
is to escape the illusion,
to be so merged with the
infinitesimal to know it
as the infinite.

SIGHT

May you see yourself
through the eyes
of your angel.

EDGE OF HER WORLD

Life had beaten her down.
So she walked to the edge of her world,
the place where solid and
liquid held hands.
It seemed to embody her story.
Her path once steady and firm
with few holes,
now a moving surface
collapsing under her weight.

In exhaustion came her silence,
and in her silence, her vision.
Each incoming wave a possibility.
Every retreat cleansing a piece of her pain.

PASSIONATE ARTIST

To watch the passionate artist
is to observe the moving hand
of the universe.

EMERGE

And one day we emerge,
fragile and beautiful
with the backdrop of the sun,
a beauty some will not see
and others will reflect.
Fortunate are we
if one of the latter,
for we are brief,
facing the winds of life,
to someday be scattered
where others will emerge.

FIRE ESCAPE

I fled the fire that led me here,
and here led me through the flames.

A power bigger and all at once me,
a source called thousands of names.

BLESSED

The stars twinkled the night's goodbye,
the earth reached out for the sun's first light,
the trees sang in welcome,
and I was blessed by another day
to see it all.

HOST

Ego urges us to live for the moment.
Spirit invites us to live in it.

JUDGMENT

Judgment is an evaluation of another's actions,
be it ten years or ten seconds ago.
The one who judges is living in their
fantasy of another's life,
rather than the present moment
reality of their own.

HAIKU: CHARACTER

What if the greatest
display of character is
choosing forgiveness?

HAIKU: INSULTS

The insults you fire
are but arrows at the moon,
my true self untouched.

HAIKU: OTHER SIDE

In a dream, I died.
There, I saw the other side.
Fear is gone for good.

HAIKU: VALUABLE

From above, so small,
but not insignificant.
Truly, you matter.

POSSIBILITIES

Just through the fires of fear,
courage melts into love,
revealing a whole new world
of possibilities.

OFFSPRING

Disquiet,
always the spawn of thought.
Peace,
ever the child of being.

ALTAR

I took the stones that had been
hurled at me and built an altar.
There,
I gave thanks to the ones who,
through it all,
never left my side.

CHILD REDISCOVERED

A child used to live in this body,
knowing only the joy of this moment,
then the next.

The forces that tried to banish the child
have not succeeded.

A light cannot be severed
by the weapons of time.

And so I hear an occasional stirring
from my innermost being.

The child lives
and waits to be rediscovered.

STRENGTH

The things the ego considers weak
are often the purest expressions
of true strength.

PATH

In countless different ways,
we travel one path of transformation,
not changing from a being that we are
into another being,
but awakening to a higher true self
that from the beginning has
permeated our entirety,
beyond the physical senses,
a unique expression of
and one with the universe.

TIME

On, on time, as if you existed,
a ghost not to be fenced,
a raging river to row against,
a fate to be lived or resisted.

DECISION

A moment of decision,
to discourage or encourage,
to tear down, deceived by ego,
to build up, guided by spirit,
the choice not reflecting the subject,
but a glimpse into the decider,
a moment of darkness or light.

FLAVORS

Swallow this moment
be it bitter or sweet.
It is the essence of life.
It is love in its magnificent
array of flavors.

ALONE

By myself is a choice.
Alone is an illusion.

ASLEEP

And then,
as if magically startled awake,
I realized I had been lost
in thoughts of things past
and things future,
asleep in places
far from my home.

LIGHT

The world needs the
light of your creation,
not the cloud of your past.

SONGS

Ego whispers of missed opportunities.
Spirit sings of new life beginnings
in each moment.

THEATER

Chasing thoughts,
we are but tiny actors
on an immense and fading stage.

Centered in presence,
we are the actors,
audience, and theater
in an immortal play.

LISTENING

Listening is an art that requires
attention over talent,
spirit over ego,
others over self.

GRATITUDE

It is in moments of gratitude
that we stand in the light of the divine.

YES, YOU

What if your smile is
Is their light today?

What if your touch
is their reminder of love?

What if your encouragement
is the sound their spirit craves?

They are out there
and they need you.

Yes, you.

SILENT RINGS

All that we gather will be
silent rings on withered hands,
but our love will live on in
many hearts yet unborn.

TWINKLE OF CRAZY

There was an uncharacteristic
twinkle of crazy in her eyes
when she looked at me.

How could I resist such a thing?

MULTIPLY

Sit with me in a quiet place
to share the beauty of this day,
to multiply the magic
in which we dwell,
and divide any
sorrow by two.

KNOW

It's all in there. I know it.
I sometimes forget,
but always know.

CIRCLE

Sometimes frail and imperfect,
we find our circle broken,
missing the measure to make it whole.
Cursed and blessed with
choices along the path,
the waves of grief and joy
lap ever at our shores,
and rarely do we know
which next will wash the sand.
But if our teary eyes and tattered hearts
remain awake and hopeful,
something beyond us shows
us love that we cannot comprehend,
and gifts us with another chance
to make our circle whole again.

ALL

You draw from me my very best,
my all, yet still I am more
than when you began.

MAZE

Another day in the
Maze of the strange,
Bending the mind,
Enticing the imagination,
Running memories of
Love and pain,
Yearning for return.

HIDING PLACES

She is gone,
but the picture of her kiss
remains on the canvas of my mind
and in the hiding places
of my heart.

NAME

All my life I have heard my name,
but never as it sounds drifting from your lips.

LEAP OF FAITH

Is there a greater leap of faith
than to leave your thoughts behind,
to silence the noise feigning real,
and live from beyond the mind?

ANGEL

What angel comes with tidings glad
and gifted wings to give us flight,
to sweep the sorrows from our minds,
and cast our demons to the night?

BRIDGE TO BEAUTIFUL

Slowly exhale,
leave yesterday in its place,
lace your fingers into mine,
and cross with me the
bridge to beautiful.

GHOSTS

The ghosts of our past
come without invitation,
movies replayed on the
screens of our minds,
sweltry through the
flames of fear,
warped by the
magnifying glass
of time.

INVISIBLE

Show me the part of you that
only the angels can see,
something I cannot
grasp with my hands
or describe with my words,
uniquely you,
and I can only know it
with the invisible part of me.

WONDER

If you spend your life walking
someone else's path,
you have lived a fragile lie,
rejecting all the wonder
the universe had planned
just for you.

YOU KNOW

You know exactly when to
touch the small of my back,
and how to softly say it's okay,
and one thousand other things
that only you have risked
enough to learn about me.

HIGH ROAD

The high road can be narrow and bumpy,
but the view is magnificent.

LOOKING

You caught me looking.

In the past I would have
turned away quickly, embarrassed,
rationalizing that you didn't see.

This time was different.

A moment of recognition,
and then it was you who turned away,
but with a knowing and intrigued smile.

TIME BETWEEN

Until I see you again,
on this side or that,
know my heart is yours
in all the time between.

BOOK

She was a mystery.
Intriguing, frightening.
A book that kept me awake
in the dark hours.
Magic floating from each page,
clouded by the looming end.
Searching for another volume
and my character alive in her story.
Restless to know everything,
anything, nothing, as long as
her haunting would linger.

PHILOSOPHY UPSIDE DOWN

I think,
therefore I suffer.

I am present,
therefore I am.

ACCEPTED

The moment she accepted herself
just as she was,
her eyes were opened to
all she could be.

DREAMS

Dreams meet across the distance,
connecting hearts while flesh is far,
painting pictures not remembered,
but alive in the mist,
waiting to take form.

COURAGEOUS EXPRESSONS

Together they decided to be wild—
not in reckless attempts
to satisfy ego desires,
but in courageous expressions
of love.

TRANSPORTED

Maybe the thing I love most about you
is the unique way you bring me
into the present.
With just a smile, glance, or soft touch,
I am transported to the only
moment that is real,
the only moment that matters,
the place where love makes its home.

LAST CHANCE

We never know when
it may be our last chance
to put someone first,
to set aside the things
that seem to matter,
and give ourselves to
the things that do.
Not to lose the love in death,
but to live the death
of life without that love.

LAYERS

There was more to her
than it seemed.
Much more.
Layer over layer.
Some even she did
not know existed.

LOST

And then, as if magically
startled awake,
I realized I had been
lost in thoughts of
things past and
things future,
asleep in places
far from my home.

DEVOUR

He crept into her heart
seeking to devour her,
but he was the one
consumed.

PERCEPTION AND REALITY

Let them think of you as they wish.
Let them speak of you as they must.
Their perception is not your reality.

GIFTED

Each moment,
the universe extends to us
the most rare and priceless
gift there is.
Always free.
Always now.

SIMPLY BEAUTIFUL

Then I saw her without
all the things they had
convinced her she must
have to be pretty.

She was simply beautiful.

UNCOMMON LOVE

There were so many
differences that few understood.
But what they had in common was an
uncommon love.
And that eclipsed all else.

NO WORDS

There are a thousand ways to say
I love you.
Most of them use no words.

WOLF

She is a wolf
with a heart so big
and a spirit so strong
that the moon stops
to howl at her.

PLAYFUL DREAMER

Playful dreamer,
Worthy and wild,
Delightful being,
Heart of a child,
Smiles in darkness,
Laughs in light,
Earthly moments,
Heavenly sight.

FREQUENCY

She lives at the frequency of love,
and there I always find her.

STRESS DEMYSTIFIED

Stress is the distance between
where our thoughts carry us
and where our lives happen.

GHOST

You are the ghost that fills my dreams,
shocking me awake,
heart thumping,
adrenaline rushing,
sweat beading,
praying to go back to sleep
to be haunted again.

FAULTS

May the one you love speak kindly of
your faults and of your courage
to admit them.

NORMAL

I don't want normal.
I want you.

PLAYFUL ANGELS

Together they
traveled paths never before tread,
opened unseen doors,
and laughed with playful angels.

TASTE OF ETERNITY

In what seemed like a moment,
the two became one.
Their love could not
be measured by time.
It was but a delicious
taste of eternity.

SO MUCH

Love her so much that she
might doubt your sanity...

...but never your passion.

FLAMES

If somehow I could swallow
the fire of your pain
and live it as my own,
know without doubt,
in an instant I would.

But since in this realm
it cannot be done,
take my hand and we'll walk
through the flames together.

ALWAYS BEEN

You say you have changed.

I say you are just beginning
to see the beauty of what
you've always have been.

AUTHOR

She read each page over and over,
in every chapter and volume,
searching for her happy ending.

Finally, weary from the search,
her eyes were drawn
to the author line.

It was her name there all along.

EGO, SPIRIT

Ego whispers of missed opportunities.
Spirit sings of new life beginnings
in each moment.

WARM THE CHILL

A gentle touch from a
long-awaited love can
warm the chill of a
thousand lonely days.

LANGUAGE

There is no special language of love,
because love is the universal language.
Often silent or misspoken, it remains,
waiting for a word or touch
to give it flight,
always landing on
another heart.

PAIN AND JOY

The pain of missing you
is a beautiful reminder of
the joy of loving you.

ALIVE AGAIN

The dark night of the mind was
pierced by the bright light of the soul,
shadows scattered on life's shore,
washed by the waves of time,
new sand, fresh dreams,
awake, alive again.

ALWAYS AND BEST

There was no sound at all,
just something in that one
hug that whispered,
"I love you always and best."

ENOUGH

Never say,
"I must not have been enough."
You were born enough and
your light grows stronger each day.
Some have just slipped too far into
their own darkness to see it.

REVELATION

Reveal the truth beneath my lie,
the part of me I can't deny,
the rusty hinges on creaking doors,
I've tried so long to ignore.
Your searing light frightens me so,
exposing ghosts I do not know.
Can this be me? I dared to ask.
No, you said, it's just your past.
I love you now, you said to me,
for your true self and all we'll be.

SOUND OF THE MOON

So they danced to the sound of the moon,
moving as one to the spin of the earth,
tasting each soft breeze,
gently alive in the presence of love.

WONDERFUL MOMENT

Sometimes there is a wonderful moment
when you stop thinking about
what is missing.

There is nothing but awareness.

You look around at all there is.

Every gift that can be touched.
Every gift that cannot.

Gratitude that defies words.

And for that wonderful moment,
you just are.

HAIKU: ALL

Fire, water, and air,
from life force to matter and
back from where we came.

HAIKU: ENCOURAGEMENT

Your encouragement
could be the song that moves their
heart to dance again.

HAIKU: MUSIC AND COLOR

You are the music
in my words and the color
in my vivid dreams.

HAIKU: MELT WITH YOU

Melt with you on a
sunny day or melt with you
on a chilly night.

NEW PEAK

A promise each sunrise
to look for beautiful surprises,
treasures always there,
but never before seen,
sounds once hidden
by the mind's sullen hum,
people with lessons
otherwise missed,
life from a new peak.

UNCHANGED

I look into the mirror,
and there the beauty and pain,
whatever my mind chooses to see,
my true self remains unchanged.

SILENCE

When came the silence of feeling most alone,
she realized that she never was.

SANITY

I love you to the point of insanity.
But in the realm of love,
who declared sanity
a virtue?

GUILT

Never in the history of humankind
has guilt changed the thing about
which one feels guilty.

SEEN AND UNSEEN

I love all of you that I can see.
I'm in love with what I cannot.

IMAGINARY DEMON

I refuse to sell my soul to the imaginary demon
who lives only in the dark recesses
of my fear.

TRUE SELF

In the midst of the physical world
and all its distractions,
remember that your true self
is a spiritual being.

AWARENESS

The simplest things done with
awareness are infinitely more
meaningful than the most
elaborate things done without
awareness.

ALL THE MORE

I embody perfection,
while being imperfection personified.
You see me as both,
and love me all the more.

NEXT VERSE

Wide eyes,
Racing heart,
Shallow breath,
Warm pen,
Your image,
All-consuming,
Oh, the next verse...

SWEETLY

Sleep sweetly tonight, my love.
Have dreams of wonderful things to come.
Awaken beside me to share their mystery.
Together we will make them real.

REFLECTED

It was one of those rare days when
the sky and the ground held hands
and reflected one another.

TIMING

The universe's timing is independent
of our egos' preferences.

FOGGY GLASS

On the foggy glass,
she drew a heart that was whole
to remind the broken one inside her
of what she once was and of
what she will be once again.

NEVER FADED

It has been such a long time,
and things have changed,
and we have changed,
but there's something
indescribable inside
that has never faded.

PICTURE

Not a day goes by that I
don't look at your picture
and smile,
or cry,
or both.

SILENT DREAMS

I love just being with you.

Especially during the simple times.

No plans, no noise.

Just us doing nothing.

Holding hands.

Sharing silent dreams.

BUTTERFLY EPILOGUE

She has wings and so she sings
the words of a different song.

Grateful for the woven womb
that set her spirit free.

To live.

To fly.

To love.

To be.

FLOWS

You have loved me enough to see
through my innumerable flaws
and into the heart that flows
gently with yours.

LAST THING

I once thought she is
the last thing I need.
Now the last thing I need
is the first thing on
my mind every morning,
all I want beside me each night,
and everything on my heart
in all the time between.

Now I know she'll be
the last thing I need.

INFINITE

We see ourselves and our world
from the captivity of spatial
relations and time orientation.
When we free ourselves of
these voluntary confinements,
we are awakened to know that the
universe within ourselves is as infinite
as the universe without.

ASHES

The ashes she blew from her wounded
heart were fairy dust upon which
her dreams would dance.

FAVORITE SHIRT

I found my favorite shirt today.
It had been missing for a long time—
probably not as long as it seemed.
It was at the bottom of a pile of clothes,
turned inside out.
I had overlooked it several times in my search.
I had seen it, touched it,
not realizing it was with me all along.

Things look different from the inside.

INSPIRATIONAL PEOPLE

The universe sends us inspirational people
not to have us become them,
but to move us to become all we are
designed to be.

CANVAS

In the art of listening,
Presence is the canvas.

VAST

Her possibilities were vast.
Something inside her knew it
and was excited.
It whispered to her heart,
which responded with a song
she never had heard.
No sheet music.
No discernable lyrics.
All she could do was dance along
with eyes read for wonder.

WHO?

"Who are you?" she asked,
as if he'd ever known the answer to this
mysteriously simple question.

REDISCOVERED

A child used to live in this body,
knowing only the joy of this moment,
then the next.
The forces that tried to banish
the child have not succeeded.
A light cannot be severed
by the weapons of time.
And so I hear an occasional
stirring from my innermost being.
The child lives and waits
to be rediscovered.

BEAUTIFUL

You know that I think you are beautiful.
Now I search for the words to
help you see all the beauty that is you,
a vision not through my eyes,
but from a place of knowing
deep within yourself.

ISLAND

An instant ago,
a memory.

An instant from now,
a guess.

The infinitesimal flash,
our island.

All else an illusion
viewed from its shore.

FEAR

This fear that marked the end of life
came not in the hours
of the heart's last beating,
but while sunlight beamed
through limbs on the horizon,
and the earth was
something to run upon.

IMPERFECT

You are not perfect.
Please never change.
You embrace imperfection with
a joy that delights my spirit.
For that, I am forever grateful.

FORM

You sensed the invisible
good in me and reached
through my walls
to give it form.

WORTH

You are worth loving.
Life is worth living.
Don't give up on either.

CURTAIN

The vision of your touch,
the smell of your skin,
the awareness of divine,
all in the realm of
one conscious breath,
a black curtain drawn on
the noise of the day.

WHITE NOISE

All the distractions became
white noise in this mysterious
vacuum of attraction.

INTERTWINE

We each come into the world
with a unique purpose.
Perhaps yours and mine
will someday intertwine.

NEW SUNRISE

Sitting alone at dawn,
staring at the shattered
mirror of her dreams,
a flicker of light startled her eye,
reflecting the warmth of hope,
and another,
and another,
and her spirit began to hum,
and her heart galloped
to the new sunrise.

BLEND

You've been too long in weary flight,
come let our hearts and spirits blend,
holding so tightly that no light
dare sneak between our skin.
No way to know my start,
or to find the ending of you,
as if we shared the same blood,
one heart;
feeling, finding,
we do.

OBSTACLE

I had traveled the same path for so long,
until I came upon an obstacle blocking the way.
I pushed with all my might, to no avail.
I refused to go back or to die there.
Left only with the choice to veer into the dark woods,
I entered.
Trembling, running, falling,
bruised and bloodied, I went on,
finally emerging in a lovely meadow
with a mountain at its edge.
I now dwell at its peak,
Ever grateful for the obstacle.

LIGHTNING

A dream to vibrate so strongly
as to walk on clouds,
to jump from one to another,
shaking free the rain,
and in one tremendous stomp,
pound out a lightning bolt.

MYSTICAL LADDER

I kissed your scars and gave thanks for mine.
Pieced together,
they formed a mystical ladder
that we both climbed
to find each other.

SPECIAL

For the first time, she felt truly special.
She did not know if it would be the last,
so she clutched the moment in her heart
for as long as it would live.
Still, slowly, it leaked away.
Time, without prejudice,
erodes both pain and bliss.
But somewhere in a place her mind
could not grasp, that feeling lived on,
hidden in the memory of
the one who made her feel.

IN DREAMS

In dreams I feel you,
your energy calling out,
unconscious hunger,
reaching, magnetic, lifting,
pulling to become one
greater than the two,
racing to awaken
all silent suppression
before sleep is burned
by the morning sun.

WORDS

Our words float into
the darkness of space,
and where they land, if ever,
remains a question unanswered.
But for the rare few,
the stars move to catch their voices
and float them back to us
to fill our finest dreams and
fuel our highest aspirations.

KEY

Blame no one else for your place in life,
and thereby give them the lock and key,
leaving fate not in your hands,
but the will of another to set you free.

COFFEE

She sits on folded legs partly covered
by the shirt she took from him,
hair a mess,
cool hands hugging coffee,
steam rising around her face
as the mug touches her cautious lips,
and the sun takes its place behind her.

POETRY

Poetry is a passage to another dimension,
be it for a moment,
or a lifetime.

HAIKU: GATE

The gate is one to
heaven and hell and to each
we carry the key.

HAIKU: TIME

On, on time as if
you existed, a sleek ghost
never to be fenced.

HAIKU: SENSES

Sight, sound, touch, taste, smell,
each an opportunity
to bask in presence.

HAIKU: SOMETIMES

This strange, awesome life.
We look forward, we look back,
and sometimes we see.

LEAPT

With eyes like moons and heart the sun,
she leapt without map or pause,
desire so strong it moved the tides,
and islands rose up to catch her.

ENGULF

Those moments when my eyes are alive,
my heart is spacious,
and my hope balances deftly at its peak,
may all the love radiating
through me and from me engulf you softly,
securely, no matter the distance between,
and draw you to me once again.

LIMITATIONS

You are under no obligation
to accept the limitations
others have assigned to you.

MISSED

What I have missed in life
are not the things I have not
done or the places I have not been,
but the things I have done and
the places I have been while
my awareness was somewhere else.

PURPOSE

Sometimes in life,
no matter how much it may hurt,
we must realize that not everyone
will accept us just as we are.
The challenge is to acknowledge their
perception for what it is,
while continuing to be true
to ourselves and our purpose.

SOFTNESS

So often, the most powerful
expression of strength is softness.

PASSION

From the passion
Comes the peace,
From the peace
Comes the sleep,
From the sleep
Comes the dream,
From the dream
Comes the passion.

FLAME

You are the candle that lights
the darkness of my life.
I will protect your flame
with all my being.

BEAUTY

Your heart knows what true beauty is,
because in your heart
is where true beauty lives.

STRANGELY YOU

Missing something,
Arms empty but open,
Looking for a sign,
Longing for a word,
Oddly enthralled,
Reason aside,
You, strangely you.

YOUR TURN

I have been here all along,
waiting for you,
the key always ready.
one simple motion,
and you are in.
It's your turn.

EMBRACE

They emptied their hands of judgment
so they could embrace love.

HUGGED

You came up behind me and hugged
me for no reason at all,
and my mind became flooded with
all the reasons why I love you.

SCARY

Scary, in a beautiful way, when
you look at me like that.

ALL THE WHILE

Worries weigh, illusions flow,
and memories leave their scar,
and all the while
we are so much more
than our thoughts of who we are.

INSTANT

In an instant her dreams were gone...

...not lost in the abyss of hope,
but transformed into her new reality.

STUCK

She's out of her mind
and stuck in my head,
and I don't see
either changing.

MOON

Why does love intensify at night?
Is it the absence of the day's distractions?
Or is it something beyond rational explanation?
Could it be the moon,
ever changing tides and moods,
drawing hearts and bodies together?

PRIVATE COLLECTION

You give me moments to write about.

Volume upon volume.

Some to share in the library of love.

And some for my private collection.

TEAR

A tear sneaks out and begins
its journey downward.
You pretend it's a drop of sweat.
They look the same.
They taste the same.
But you know the difference,
the truth.
And so do they.
It's source is not of boiling blood,
but of a shattered heart.

VESSEL

Your body is gone but your spirit lingers,
Disrupting the rhythm of my heart,
Slipping through the alleys of my brain,
Glimpses of a shadow of a ghost,
Dashing behind the next fading thought,
Disappearing mist reforming in the silence,
Always present, haunting, and inviting,
Reminding me of your essence,
Until I hold its vessel once more.

SHINE

Who knows which light will break
through the clouds onto a
life filled with rain?

Ours it not to know,
but shine, simply
shine.

FALL: TINGES

Tinges of fall in the leaves of my woods
spark life anew in the heart
of my world.

FALL: HUDDLE

The heat of summer began
to drip off the earth.
Soon, beautiful color would be
crunching beneath their feet.
And they would huddle beneath one blanket.
Living, wonderfully living.

FALL: DISPLAY

Autumn is nature's stunning display
of the beauty of death midst the
hope of the coming rebirth.

FALL: PROMISE

This year,
a spirit promise to embrace the
magnificence that is fall,
totally present,
observing every color,
feeling each breeze,
listening to the shuffling sounds,
and in silent amazement
giving thanks for it all.

FALL: FIRES

The beach was cold,
unlike the burning visions of those living inland.
So they walk with arms around each other,
blocking the outside forces,
and the wind, and the spray.

And they built fires in the sand
and their souls,
and hardly noticed the hidden sun.

SENSES

And for a moment he experienced
her with all his senses.
Simultaneously.
Shocking.
Afraid to stay.
Terrified to go.

LIFE FLOWS ON

A different river,
in a different time,
a different song,
with a different rhyme.

And life flows on.

NO ATTACHMENT

Giving the love that you are
with no attachment to the results.

YOURSELF

With me,
please just be yourself.

I have no desire to fix you.

I simply want to love you.

NOW

"Kiss me now," she said.

"It's always now," he answered.

TRUTH

Your truth will set you apart,
and so set apart,
free.

FLOWERS

She loved the flowers.
They became her camouflage.
She reflected their complexion,
absorbed their scent,
and moved her face with theirs
to the curve of the sun.

SECRETLY PRETTY

She was strong with a gentle spirit,
quietly brilliant,
and secretly pretty.

DRAGON

Our eyes dart in fear,
looking all around for the dragon.
We chase it imposters.
We hide and pretend we are hidden.
All the while,
the dragon's fire burns from within.

EDGE

You loved me when I appeared unlovable,
prickly and cold, far from the light,
lost in illusions I swore were real,
love unanswered, ignored,
seemingly wasted,
the breath at my life's fading sound
that awakened my spirit and blood,
a hand extended at the edge,
and there is hope for this
ever grateful heart.

WILD

She was wild.

Not the machinations of a petulant ego,
but the innate spirit of an angel sprite,
a mustang unsaddled,
only to be watched with
envy-sprinkled smiles.

ENTRANCED

You are the butterfly that
comes to rest on my shoulder.
I am entranced by your silent beauty,
my blood rushing beneath you.

REMEMBER

My desire is to remember...

not the days of darkness or light,

or the wrongs inflicted upon me or by me,

not the dreams realized or lost,

or even the love received or given,

...but to remember and know the part
of me that never changed
through all these.

SONG

You sensed the song trapped inside me,
reached gently through my walls,
hummed a melody into my mind,
wrote the words on my tongue,
and filled me with courage
to sing without shame.

SHE KNOWS

She knows.

Ignoring.
Pretending.
Rationalizing.
Desiring.
Denying.

But she knows.

WITHOUT WORDS

Speak to me.
Without words.
Let your eyes tell me
what you need,
what you want,
what you crave.
I will listen,
and in the same silence,
give you all you desire.

STEALING BREATH

They fell so fast,
perfect rhythm,
note for note,
landing beautifully and hard,
stealing breath,
left searching for air,
and a song to rise
and dance as one.

HERE

Your voice is the
sound that matters most.
If ever these thoughts
that flood my mind
seem to mean more,
know that they are nothing.
I am still learning,
still chasing fleeting illusions,
slowly understanding that
all I have is now
and where I belong is here.

WHISPERED

My arms whispered to me and
told me that their
favorite thing in the world
is to be wrapped around you.

REFRESHED HEART

When you entered my world,
my true self didn't change.
That part never does.
It's invisible, eternal.
But your presence has ignited my
awareness to all the wonder that is life.
So with new eyes and refreshed heart
I see who I really am and the beauty
that is you,
and I love us all the more.

HAUNTING

What do you think of when you don't
want to think of me?

What images frighten the ghosts away?

I need to know.

The haunting is overwhelming.

HIDDEN

Beneath her eyes a secret lies,
elusive now to pen and tongue,
tales for which my spirit cries,
hidden till that time shall come.

BY HEART

I like that you know my words by heart.

I love that they make you smile.

VOICE

A moment like something
in a somewhere-like sound,
her words were vanished,
but her voice was found.

BEAUTIFUL THINGS

Beautiful things come into our lives
only for a little while,
and the less time we spend judging them,
the more time we have to love them.

INTRIGUE

And then, unexpectedly,
intrigue was born,
mellow, but attentive,
emotion with a cloak,
everything seemed possible.

ICE CREAM

With butterflies in her tummy,
and ice cream on her lips,
she saw the world in
a whole new way.

EMBRACE THE BOLD

Hands reach out,
While you pull in,
Afraid to be more,
Than what you've been.

Viewing love,
Walking the mess,
Craving the more,
Living the less.

And comes the time,
You must decide,
To change the path,
Or cling to pride.

Settle not,
Reach up and hold,
Release the fear,
Embrace the bold.

DREAMING

Do not be confined to dreaming at night,
where stories are strange and memory weak,
but imagine grand in hours of light,
when pictures are formed, and watched,
and speak.

STORM

There was a storm brewing inside her.
He could see the waves breaking in her eyes.
He could hear the distant thunder in her voice.
He could feel the first rain beading on her skin.
He prayed to be the one her
lightning would strike.

TRANSFORMATION

Transformation from where you are to where
you are inspired to be begins with the
belief you can.
The belief you can begins with the
belief you are worthy.

STRANGE

When the strange becomes ordinary,
it's magic seeps out as a vapor,
searching for a new host to infuse
and manifest once again as the strange.

BUTTERFLY PRELUDE

Who chooses this odd insect
to be the architect of
such perfection?

What force guides its
flawless weaving?

It is the same power in many disguises,
moving through each stage
of transformation.

It is the love that when seen
through spirit eyes always
looks the same.

CIRCUMSTANCES

Your current life circumstances are
the result of decisions made and
actions take in the past,
be it decades or moments ago.

They are just circumstances.

They do not define you.

COUNSEL

Seek the counsel of the daring,

those who have learned through
their own pain,

when to run,

and when to reign.

RISEN

Dust off the ashes from which you have risen.
Stand in the knowledge of your worthiness.
Flood the air with your gratitude.
Declare this moment your home.

EXPERIENCE

If you only see what your ego
wants you to see,
and only hear what your ego
wants you to hear,
it is those predetermined choices,
rather than something higher,
that arrange your life experience.

FILL

Drain me of all that I was,
and fill me with all that you are.

LIST

Lost in regret,
she decided to make a list of all the
things she had changed by reliving
them in her mind.

Hours later,
she stared at a blank sheet,
and with a smile,
decided to live and love again.

FORGIVENESS

In the realm of self-healing,
the choice of forgiveness has
nothing to do with whether the
other person is sorry.
Forgiveness is not a device
to affect the behavior of
another person,
but a way to bring
peace within yourself.

CENTER

Rare is the moment when you are
not in the center of my mind.

But my mind can be so crowded that
not even its center is deserving.

You are also in the center of my heart
in a place only you can fill.

NOTHING

Sometimes the most courageous
thing to do and the most
difficult thing to say
is nothing.

LOVED

Being loved just because I'm me,
and even though I'm me.

NEVER FADE

Some things fade.
A favorite shirt washed for years.
A broken toy in seasons of sun.
Stars long ago fallen.

Some things never fade.
A smile that lights the darkness of our sorrow.
An invisible hand wiping our tears.
A spirit that glows through eternity.

SEARCH

No matter how hard I tried to hide my heart,
you always found it.

Thank you for never giving up the search.

CONNECTED

When you need me, I feel it.
Such is the way of connected hearts.

GAMBLE

An absolute gamble
in a different kind of heat,
with magic in the air,
and destiny to meet.

AWAKENING

There is a powerful moment
of awakening when we
move from thinking
that we know,
to knowing that
we think.

EACH MOMENT

Each moment is a new reality,
unlike any before it,
or any to come.

HAIKU: WAVES

They parked in the sand,
and counted the waves and dreams,
the number the same.

HAIKU: SOFT EYES

Beauty lies behind
soft eyes awake to sleeping
possibilities.

HAIKU: TRY AGAIN

Dare we try again
and risk failing and falling
worse than before? Yes.

HAIKU: HOME

It means so much to
me when my words find a home
deep inside of you.

PEACEFUL

Life can be so much more peaceful
than we make it.
It's often simply a matter of
deciding what matters.

MOMENTS

Enjoying any one of life's moments
begins with being fully present in it,
and is made special by being
grateful for it.

*Thank you for sharing these moments through words.
I am truly grateful.*

Dean Jackson

Table of Contents for "Poetry of Presence"

39   Accepted (The moment she...)
8   Age (If age is only...)
50   Alive Again (The dark night...)
32   All (You draw from...)
56   All the More (I embody...)
78   All the While (Worries weigh...)
27   Alone (By myself is...)
24   Altar (I took the...)
50   Always and Best (There was no...)
48   Always Been (You say you...)
34   Angel (What angel comes...)
2   Artist (Each now is a...)
62   Ashes (The ashes she...)
28   Asleep (And then as if...)
48   Author (She read each...)
103   Awakening (There is a...)
56   Awareness (The simplest things...)
64   Beautiful (You know that...)
94   Beautiful Things (Beautiful things come...)
76   Beauty (Your heart knows...)
17   Beyond (Things come from...)
68   Blend (You've been too...)
22   Blessed (The stars twinkled...)
38   Book (She was a...)
34   Bridge to Beautiful (Slowly exhale...)
2   Butterfly (When she transformed...)
60   Butterfly Epilogue (She has wings...)
97   Butterfly Prelude (Who chooses this...)
93   By Heart (I like that you...)
63   Canvas (In the art...)
101   Center (Rare is the moment...)
25   Child Rediscovered (A child used...)
32   Circle (Sometimes frail and...)
12   Circle of Angels (I see your...)

98   Circumstances (Your current life...)
72   Coffee (She sits on...)
102   Connected (When you need...)
98   Counsel (Seek the counsel...)
39   Courageous Expressions (Together they...)
67   Curtain (The vision of...)
27   Decision (A moment of...)
2   Depths of Her Soul (She dances to...)
42   Devour (He crept into...)
13   Direction (To look honestly...)
86   Dragon (Our eyes dart...)
96   Dreaming (Do not be...)
39   Dreams (Dreams meet across...)
103   Each Moment (Each moment...)
87   Edge (You loved me...)
20   Edge of Her World (Life had beaten...)
15   Ego Disguises (Ego comes in many...)
49   Ego, Spirit (Ego whispers...)
77   Embrace (They emptied their...)
95   Embrace the Bold (Hands reach...)
21   Emerge (And one day...)
74   Engulf (Those moments...)
51   Enough (Never say...)
88   Entranced (You are the...)
99   Experience (If you only see...)
12   Expressions (One of the...)
82   Fall: Display (Autumn is...)
83   Fall: Fires (The beach was...)
82   Fall: Huddle (The heat of...)
83   Fall: Promise (A spirit promise...)
82   Fall: Tinges (Tinges of fall...)
45   Faults (May the one...)
62   Favorite Shirt (I found my...)
65   Fear (This fear that...)
99   Fill (Drain me of...)
21   Fire Escape (I fled the...)

76   Flame (You are the...)
47   Flames (If somehow I...)
27   Flavors (Swallow this moment...)
9   Flawed (The more we talked...)
86   Flowers (She loved the...)
60   Flows (You have loved...)
58   Foggy Glass (On the foggy...)
100   Forgiveness (In the realm...)
66   Form (You sensed the...)
44   Frequency (She lives at...)
103   Gamble (An absolute...)
3   Gift from a Child (When a child...)
42   Gifted (Each moment...)
45   Ghost (You are the...)
35   Ghosts (The ghosts of...)
29   Gratitude (It is in...)
55   Guilt (Never in the history...)
53   Haiku: All
23   Haiku: Character
53   Haiku: Encouragement
73   Haiku: Gate
104   Haiku: Home
23   Haiku: Insults
53   Haiku: Melt With You
53   Haiku: Music and Color
23   Haiku: Other Side
73   Haiku: Senses
104   Haiku: Soft Eyes
73   Haiku: Sometimes
73   Haiku: Time
104   Haiku: Try Again
23   Haiku: Valuable
104   Haiku: Waves
92   Haunting (What do you think...)
91   Here (Your voice is...)
93   Hidden (Beneath her eyes...)

33	Hiding Places (She is gone...)
36	High Road (The high road...)
22	Host (Ego urges us...)
78	Hugged (You came up...)
94	Ice Cream (With butterflies...)
10	Identity (Love is what you...)
55	Imaginary (I refuse to sell...)
66	Imperfect (You are not...)
71	In Dreams (In dreams I...)
61	Infinite (We see ourselves...)
7	Inspiration (The wishes and...)
62	Inspirational People (The universe...)
79	Instant (In an instant...)
67	Intertwine (We each come...)
94	Intrigue (And then, unexpectedly...)
35	Invisible (Show me the...)
65	Island (An instant ago...)
7	It and All (Whenever you come...)
22	Judgment (Judgment is an...)
72	Key (Blame no one...)
31	Know (It's all in there...)
7	Knowing (I've come to know...)
49	Language (There is no...)
40	Last Chance (We never know...)
61	Last Thing (I once thought...)
41	Layers (There was more...)
34	Leap of Faith (Is there a...)
74	Leapt (With eyes like...)
15	Letters (We are all...)
84	Life Flows On (A different river...)
28	Light (The world needs...)
69	Lightning (A dream to...)
74	Limitations (You are under...)
100	List (Lost in regret...)
29	Listening (Listening is an...)
37	Looking (You caught me...)

41 Lost (And then, as if...)

4 Lost in Words (I'm looking at her...)

8 Love Anew (Collapse into me...)

101 Loved (Being loved...)

19 Magic (The highest form...)

4 Magician (May you become...)

33 Maze (Another day...)

11 Melody (Music is a power...)

75 Missed (What I have...)

79 Moon (Why does love...)

13 More (You are so much...)

31 Multiply (Sit with me...)

70 Mystical Ladder (I kissed your...)

33 Name (All my life...)

102 Never Fade (Some things fade...)

58 Never Faded (It has been...)

57 Next Verse (Wide eyes...)

54 New Peak (A promise each...)

68 New Sunrise (Sitting alone at...)

84 No Attachment (Giving the love...)

43 No Words (There are a...)

46 Normal (I don't want...)

101 Nothing (Sometimes the most...)

85 Now (Kiss me now...)

69 Obstacle (I had traveled...)

24 Offspring (Disquiet, always...)

14 One Day (One day...)

5 Ongoing Choice (Each moment...)

50 Pain and Joy (The pain of...)

76 Passion (From the passion...)

20 Passionate Artist (To observe the...)

19 Past (The past is but...)

26 Path (In countless...)

105 Peaceful (Life can be...)

42 Perception and Reality (Let them think...)

9 Perspective (No matter where...)

38   Philosophy Upside Down (I think...)
59   Picture (Not a day goes...)
46   Playful Angels (Together they...)
44   Playful Dreamer (Playful dreamer...)
72   Poetry (Poetry is a...)
24   Possibilities (Just through the...)
80   Private Collection (You give me...)
75   Purpose (Sometimes in life...)
64   Rediscovered (A child used...)
57   Reflected (It was one of...)
92   Refreshed Heart (When you entered...)
88   Remember (My desire is to...)
51   Revelation (Reveal the truth...)
99   Risen (Dust off the...)
55   Sanity (I love you to...)
78   Scary (Scary, in a...)
102   Search (No matter how...)
5   Searches (Ego searches...)
5   Secret (Meet me in the...)
86   Secretly Pretty (She was strong...)
55   Seen and Unseen (I love all of...)
84   Senses (And for a moment...)
89   She Knows (She knows...)
81   Shine (Who knows which...)
19   Sight (May you see...)
54   Silence (When came the...)
59   Silent Dreams (I love just...)
30   Silent Rings (All that we...)
43   Simply Beautiful (Then I saw her...)
47   So Much (Love her so...)
6   Soft Gaze (Look upon another...)
75   Softness (So often, the...)
6   Something New (Faced with inevitable...)
89   Song (You sensed the...)
28   Songs (Ego whispers of...)
52   Sound of the Moon (So they danced...)

70   Special (For the first time...)
90   Stealing Breath (They fell so fast...)
25   Strength (The things that...)
45   Stress Demystified (Stress is the...)
96   Storm (There was a storm...)
97   Strange (When the strange...)
77   Strangely You (Missing something...)
79   Stuck (She's out of...)
57   Sweetly (Sleep sweetly...)
46   Taste of Eternity (In what seemed...)
80   Tear (A tear sneaks...)
29   Theater (Chasing thoughts...)
26   Time (On, on time...)
37   Time Between (Until I see...)
58   Timing (The universe's timing...)
18   To Live (Whether I know...)
11   Trading (Just here...)
96   Transformation (Transformation from...)
40   Transported (Maybe the thing...)
10   Truce (Declare an end...)
56   True Self (In the midst...)
85   Truth (Your truth wil...)
16   Turns (What lurks or lies...)
31   Twinkle of Crazy (There was an...)
3   Two Souls (Two souls looked out...)
54   Unchanged (I looked into...)
43   Uncommon Love (There were so...)
63   Vast (Her possibilities were...)
81   Vessel (Your body is...)
93   Voice (A moment like...)
18   Walls (These towering walls...)
49   Warm the Chill (A gentle touch...)
91   Whispered (My arms whispered...)
63   Who? (Who are you...)
67   White Noise (All the distractions...)
87   Wild (She was wild...)

90   Without Words (Speak to me...)
44   Wolf (She is a...)
36   Wonder (If you spend...)
52   Wonderful Moment (Sometimes there...)
71   Words (Our words float...)
66   Worth (You are worth...)
30   Yes, You (What if your...)
36   You Know (You know...)
77   Your Turn (I have been...)
85   Yourself (With me...)